Why Living Things Need...

Food

Daniel Nunn

Heinemann Library
Chicago, Illinois

www.capstonepub.com
Visit our website to find out more information about Heinemann-Raintree books.

To order:

☎ Phone 888-454-2279
🖳 Visit www.capstonepub.com
to browse our catalog and order online.

Edited by Dan Nunn, Rebecca Rissman, and Sian Smith
Designed by Joanna Hinton-Malivoire
Picture research by Ruth Blair
Production by Victoria Fitzgerald
Originated by Capstone Global Library Ltd
Printed and bound in China by Leo Paper Products Ltd

15 14 13 12 11
10 9 8 7 6 5 4 3 2 1

Library of Congress Cataloging-in-Publication Data
Nunn, Daniel.
  Food / Daniel Nunn.
    p. cm.—(Why living things need)
  Includes bibliographical references and index.
  ISBN 978-1-4329-5914-2 (hc)—ISBN 978-1-4329-5920-3 (pb)
1. Animals—Food—Juvenile literature. 2. Plants—Nutrition—Juvenile literature. I. Title.
  QL756.5.N86 2012
  572'.4—dc23   2011014648

Acknowledgments
We would like to thank the following for permission to reproduce photographs: Corbis pp.5 (© moodboard), 6 (© Keren Su), 13 (© Stephanie Pilick/dpa), 17 (© Image Source); Photolibrary pp.12 (Buddy Mays/Flirt Collection), 14 (SMuller); Shutterstock pp.4 (© Losevsky Pavel), 7 (© margouillat photo), 8 (© Elnur), 9 (© Vaclav Volrab), 10 (© Khoroshunova Olga), 11 (© Igumnova Irina), 14 (© oksana.perkins), 15 (© Monkey Business Images), 16 (© Catalin Petolea), 18 (© Monkey Business Images), 19 (© Makarova Viktoria (Vikarus)), 20 (© Chas), 21 (© R_R), 22 (© ArjaKo's), 22 (© AISPIX), 22 (© Matti), 23 (© Makarova Viktoria (Vikarus)), 23 (© Igumnova Irina).

Front cover photograph of sheep reproduced with permission of Shutterstock (© Traveler). Back cover photograph of a cow eating grass reproduced with permission of Shutterstock (© Igumnova Irina).

We would like to thank Nancy Harris, Dee Reid, and Diana Bentley for their assistance in the preparation of this book.

Every effort has been made to contact copyright holders of any material reproduced in this book. Any omissions will be rectified in subsequent printings if notice is given to the publisher.

Contents

What Is Food?

Food is everything that we eat.

We eat lots of different foods.

Living Things and Food

People, other animals, and plants are living things.

All living things need food.

Plant Food

Plants make their own food.

Plants use water, air, and sunlight to make food.

Animal Food

Some animals eat plants.

Cows eat grass.

Some animals eat other animals.

Owls eat mice.

Some animals eat other animals
and plants.

Some people eat meat
and vegetables.

Why Do Living Things Need Food?

People and other animals need food to stay alive.

Plants need food to stay alive, too.

Food gives living things energy.

Living things need energy to move.

Living things need energy to
keep warm.

Living things need energy to grow.

Food Quiz

Which of these things does not need food?

22

Answer on page 24

Picture Glossary

energy the power to do things. Living things need energy to move, keep warm, and grow.

living thing something that is alive, such as an animal or a plant

Index

Answer to question on page 22
The cat and the girl need food.
The wall does not need food.

Notes for parents and teachers

Before reading
Ask the children to tell you their favorite food. Write their suggestions on paper to make a poster. Ask the children why they think it is important to eat food. Add their ideas to the poster. Explain why all living things need food. If the children are ready, discuss food chains. Plants make their own food and so are at the start of all the food chains.

After reading
- Cut out pictures of animals, including people, and paste them onto pieces of construction paper. Do the same with pictures showing foods those animals would eat. Ask each child to choose an animal card. Lay out the food cards face up and tell the children to take turns to select a food their animal would eat. If they cannot see a suitable card, ask them to suggest a food and write this onto a new piece of card. Discuss their choices.
- Divide the cards above into "food" and "animal" piles. Give one child the animal cards and another the food cards. The children should take turns flipping over a card from their pile. They should call out "Snap!" if the animal would eat the food shown. The first child to call out correctly takes the matching pair. The winner is the child with the most pairs after all the cards have been turned over.